"You Will Never Amount to Sh*t!"

by

Kiah Nyame

An Autoethnography of Transforming
Trauma to Triumph:
One Man's Journey Towards Healing

Copyright © Kiah Nyame 2019

All Rights Reserved

ISBN: 978-1-7324781-2-1

Editing: Wandah Gibbs, Ed. D.,

         Gina Petschke M.A.

First Edition

Printed in the United States

WGW Publishing Inc. Rochester, NY

For my sons, Tyrick, James, and Jaquan.
They are my consistent motivation for
doing this work...

FOREWARD

Kiah Nyame's amazing memoir tells the story of an African American man growing up in Rochester New York besieged by the social ills common to far too many black families. Kiah was born into poverty and struggle and recounts a single childhood wish and desire . . . to please his mother. Lacking the physical, mental or emotional resources to raise a family, his mother sought assistance from Social Services and this resulted in him spending years in foster care where he received a fragile and fleeting stability. Still, Kiah held out hope of his mother returning to get him but he would be 13 years of age before being permanently reunited with her.

The question which emerged in the heart and mind of Kiah as a child suffering unspeakable abuse, beginning in foster and continuing throughout his life was, "Why doesn't my mother love me" and later questioning the 'goodness' of religion or a God that did not rescue an innocent child and who used His wrath to punish. He found ways to cope with his suffering by following the examples of high rollers, the usual urban suspects, the hustlers, pimps, gangsters, and drug dealers. These ill-gained role models displayed all of the material success that Kiah had longed for throughout his life, sex, cars, clothes, and women.

School was a major disappointment growing up black in Rochester. It was a teacher from school that told him he would never amount to much nor could he measure up as a black boy, to the white idea of success. Soon he resorted to crime, using and selling drugs, acting out violently, and ultimately becoming addicted to alcohol and drugs.

But this is not simply a story about the struggles of a young black man trying to survive the tumultuous social ills of urban America. Instead, this is a testimony to one man's steadfast courage and search for truth and understanding, a kinder, healthier and just life. Having arrived at a crossroad after causing harm to those he loved, Kiah embraced his past; his wrongs and his moments of clarity eventually arriving at a place of transformation and healing. His journey led him back to school, his community and his family. Now, Dr. Kiah Nyame has studied and learned about the role that his racial socialization and multigenerational history played on his *own* life experiences and how past events have shaped his behaviors and indeed the behaviors of African Americans as a group.

This is not a book for the faint of heart or those who desire to ignore the truth about what life is 'really' like growing up black, poor, and abused; the plight of the less fortunate. It is a book for anyone seeking to understand human resilience in the face of seemingly insurmountable obstacles including; severe trauma, poverty, and oppression.

The reader will be guided through Dr. Nyame's brilliant analysis of historical cultural values and theories of development in light of past and present parenting practices and community culture. Kiah lets you into his heart and mind, introducing you to the boy, the son, the brother, the father and the warrior!

-Dr. Joy DeGruy

Author: *Post Traumatic Slave Syndrome*

CHAPTER ONE

The Beginnings

Once upon a time a baby boy was born into a traumatic situation. Wait! I can't even begin in this manner because my beginnings, though not stereotypical, were common for African American children born in the South during that time in history. In fact, it was a recurring theme for African American children to be abused by their parents under the curtain of "I love you". One must understand that many parents only raised their children using the information that was passed down to them. The behavioral practices of discipline and socialization were taught to their great-grandparents via their experiences on the plantation. And we know that even after emancipation, the injuries to the community continued, causing a trickle down effect.

I was first told that I was born in Anderson, South Carolina. I was born in 1962 at the height of the Civil Rights

Movement in America. I have been told several versions about how I arrived in Rochester, New York. One story is that my mom abandoned me home alone and moved to Rochester, leaving me hungry and crying. Apparently, I was only about six months old. Another story was that I was left with family. I may never know the complete truth. This in and of itself is traumatic as I often wonder what happened and why I was abandoned to live with family members I have no recollection of. I often wonder about my early days and it is a recurring source of frustration and insecurity.

One story, as told to me by my uncle, is that I was brought as a baby (nothing but a huge head I'm told) from Anderson to Rochester by bus, screaming and crying all the way. My earliest memories of childhood are at my grandmother's house which was located directly behind a big church on Lyndhurst Street. I don't recall many interactions with my mother or grandmother prior to five years of age.

2

As traumatic as my beginnings were, there are countless, similar stories that today seem inconceivable. It should be noted however that even after slavery was abolished in the United States, traumatic events and experiences continued. Along came debt slavery also known as debt servitude where an employer compelled a worker to pay off a debt with work. Though peonage was outlawed by Congress in 1867, it continued, then was followed by the Jim Crow era. The injuries never stopped and the wounds are often transferred from generation to generation.

To this day, one can be out in the community or at the local shopping center and hear a parent call their toddler "stupid", "the N word", and other derogatory names. Added to this is the parent's constant worry about their child being kidnapped or killed while out and about.

CHAPTER TWO
Trauma

My first incident of trauma happened at Mother's house. One day a young lady was babysitting me. I recall being stripped of my clothing and her removing her clothing too. She began to fondle me and play with my penis. Then she laid down on the couch or bed and demanded that I get on top of her. To this day I can't describe any feelings that I may have had. I didn't know that what was happening was inappropriate and I think I believed we were playing a game or something. I only remember that it happened.

Not long after this incident, we moved to a very tall building, which I later learned, was the Hanover Projects. These projects comprised of a group of seven buildings each seven stories high and located a little less than a mile from our old house. As I recall, the building we lived in always smelled like urine in the stairwell and hallways. People were often seen with needles in their arms on the roof of the building. But despite the constant smell of urine in the hallways and the rats in the basement, this was home.

Being that I was only about five years old, I did what children of that age do; I played a lot. I was always playing on the elevator. I was constantly on the elevator pushing the buttons for people. This sometimes earned me pennies or a nickel and I would run off to the store located in an adjacent building to buy candy.

Sometime later, I remember riding in a car with a white woman. We eventually pulled up to a house quite a distance from Hanover Projects, where I was left with strangers. I didn't understand why I couldn't return home. I was told I would be staying there. What went on in that particular place is a nothing but a blur though I do remember Mother coming to pick me up every so often for a visit and taking me to Carroll's

Restaurant (now known as Burger King) to eat.

I can't explain to you the pain I endured when I realized that Mom hadn't actually come to take me home with her. I didn't yet have the capacity to understand why she wanted me to stay with these people. Also, it wasn't until much later that I would realize I internalized the trauma that resulted from my feelings of abandonment.

Approximately a year later I was once again picked up by a white woman then driven to another home. I remember clearly the first time I saw the large pink house. It is etched into my mind like it was yesterday. Little did I know that I was on a journey to experience several ongoing, traumatizing events while in this house.

CHAPTER THREE

Foster Care

Because this is not a work in which I intend to demonize or belittle the character of anyone, whether alive or dead, I will not use any names. Today I believe these people did their best to foster me, though as you will see, their best was often not helpful in the least.

When I arrived at the pink house, there were three other foster boys living there. These three boys were actually brothers. So, again, I had feelings of not belonging. Questions consumed me: "Why weren't my brothers with me? What is it about me that mom doesn't like? Am I different from my mother's other children? Why, why, why?" These questions would haunt and direct my behavior for many years to come.

The adults in this house were essentially good-hearted people. The mother stayed home with the children, and the father worked at the local international production factory. One positive thing I recall is that we always had plenty to eat and good clothes to wear. I remember attending Mt. Vernon church and going to school. Also, we were allowed to play in the back yard and go to the playground. To the outside world, it appeared that I was living the life of a typical seven-year-old boy, however, what went on inside the house was a completely different story. The household was filled with physical and emotional abuse.

We were a family who went to church all day on Sunday and several times during the week. We boys were eventually groomed to be gospel singers. We were taught songs to sing, and because I have a decent voice, I was chosen as the group leader. They dressed us in identical suits for our performances and I remember wearing a sherbet colored outfit on at least one occasion. We looked like authentic entertainers. I have always wondered if this had something to do with the Jackson Five coming onto the scene. I was put out front, while the other guys were my backup singers. Also, we learned showmanship, and there were times I felt proud to be part of this group. I enjoyed being the lead singer because, I got more attention and compliments than the others, though more whippings too, or so it seemed.

It wasn't long before we were performing at other churches, revivals, and other venues. We travelled a bit too to perform in small towns outside Rochester. It really made me feel good to be a part of making people smile. All I could think was that people really liked me when I was performing. This was the beginning of years of doing things to please people. I especially wanted to please my mother and then, maybe, she would take me back home. I believed that if I sung well and learned as much as I could about the Bible, Mom would be proud of me.

Though to the public we appeared to be the perfect little family, behind closed doors, the songs we performed were literally beaten into us. We were struck each time we didn't sing a note just right or the way the woman of the house wanted it to sound. We were beaten with everything from wooden spoons to electrical appliance cords. Our training was very physical in nature, demanding, and hurtful. When we didn't say the words of a song correctly, or we talked back or chose to have an opinion, we were given a large wooden spoon filled with-Castor Oil. Many of the beatings and other abuse disguised as discipline were painful and extremely scary. I have many scars both physical and mental dating back from that time.

Some of you can identify, and the rest don't have to think very hard to imagine the fear instilled in us as children. This resulted in me growing up thinking that the way to get others to do what I wanted them to do was to instill the same type of fear in them. For years I too resorted to confronting others with a weapon of some sort.

CHAPTER FOUR

Grown Folks Business

After about two years or so, the three brothers who lived with me in foster care were returned to their mother's house. This was a time when children were not allowed to ask questions about "grown folks business." I was not allowed an opportunity to understand nor to work through the loss I was feeling. All I know is I felt all alone and deeply sad. Once again I was consumed with questions: "Why hasn't my mom come to get me? Why hasn't she been to see me? Doesn't she love me?"

I am not sure for how long I remained the only child in the house, but it wasn't that long before two more brothers moved in. During that time, we didn't do much singing, however, I was now being told that I was destined to be a preacher when I grew up. In an effort to teach me the stories of the Bible and for me to be able to repeat those stories, the abuse continued.

I delivered sermons on youth Sundays, a eulogy at a baby's funeral, and led religious programs. Yet, for some reason, as much as I loved God, something never felt quite right. I had a lot of unanswered questions about God. And if I dared question the scriptures, swift physical action took place instead because, "You don't question God." What was brewing psychologically and emotionally wouldn't be uncovered until many years later and only after the survival of several other traumatic experiences.

Three or four months later, another young man moved into the foster home. He was a sibling to the other two brothers that had recently replaced the ones who'd left. There were some rumors circulating that this brother liked boys.

Though I'd heard older boys talking at the playground and recreation centers about having sex, smoking cigarettes, and reefer, I was fearful of sex as a topic and had not yet talked to anyone about it. I tried to act cool by pretending I was experienced, but I didn't have a clue about what they were talking about. I also learned how to fight, how to know when I couldn't win and to run instead!

After this third brother moved into the house, the environment took a shift. On the surface the beatings, church attendance, and the gospel singing continued, however, during the night there was a whole lot more going on. Sexual exploration had begun. The boy rumored to like boys came to me one night and a sexual encounter took place. This felt good and allowed me to forget about the conditions in the home. Early on I would resort to all kinds of behavior to escape my reality. Escapism continued through my early 30s. However, after learning more about my sexuality I used girls, alcohol, drugs, and anger as escape routes. I have always felt and thought that what we were doing was wrong and nasty. Yet, it didn't take long before I became addicted to the feeling and began to enjoy these encounters. Later I would find out that I was pre-disposed to becoming addicted to many things.

I don't think our foster parents ever knew what was going on at night between us boys. If they had known, we would've surely been beaten, especially since our foster parents were very strict, no nonsense religious people. This type of behavior was truly taboo. Getting away with it felt better to me than the behavior itself. Though I was only 10 or 11 years of age at the time, these experiences started what would be a lengthy span in my life of lying, deceit, and manipulation. Somehow it felt good to rebel against the things I had been taught.

CHAPTER FIVE

Contradictory Messages

I always believed that religious information was in contradiction. The God I knew about, who loved me, had a mean, negative side. After all, He could destroy the world and kill for the Israelites. If it was okay for God to be both loving and hateful, then why couldn't I? "Heck, I'm so bad Mama doesn't even want me!"

After about 10 months from the time this third brother moved in, his two brothers moved out. I am not sure if they went back home or not. I began to feel some type of closeness and empathy for the remaining brother. After all, his brothers were gone and he was left in this foster home just like me. The problem was, because of his behavior and what I thought about it, I couldn't risk showing any weakness. I didn't want him to know I felt his pain. We couldn't even encourage nor console each other.

The boys were soon replaced with two more brothers from yet another family. Not much changed besides the faces and personalities. The sexual exploration continued. The beatings and other abuse continued as well. While I developed an individual relationship with each of the boys who shared the foster home with me, it should be noted that they have their stories and this is mine...

Eventually my foster family moved from the pink house to a much better home a few miles away. The place was beautiful and we were taught to keep it clean and well groomed. Inside the house we boys did all the chores. Outside yard work during summer was led by the foster mom. The snow removal was also our job. During my approximate six years living in this family, I learned to clean walls; base-boards with a cloth and toothbrush; to cut grass with a hand-mower; and to pull weeds. These skills would prove useful later in life.

Between my late fourth and early fifth year of living in this foster home,

Mom began to visit me more frequently starting with every 2 weeks then every week as part of a transition plan for me to return to live with her. Even with all my pent-up anger and feelings of abandonment, I was always excited to see her and spend time with her. Again, we would often go to Carroll's or McDonalds, and it felt good to be with Mom. I felt like I belonged to something and someone.

Soon I would start to spend weekends at home with my mom and my brothers. Mom still lived in the Hanover housing projects. One thing I noticed when I returned to the projects was that most of the fathers were never around. Not that it bothered me a whole lot then, since not seeing moms with dads was part of the norm in Hanover.

CHAPTER SIX

A Much Different World

The Hanover projects exhibited a much different world than I had experienced with my foster family. While living at the Hanover projects, it was normal to see the older guys and girls on the roof of the building having parties, smoking reefer, and drinking. They appeared to be having a lot of fun. However, it was also normal to see couples and groups of people fighting, and all out violence was a common occurrence. Soon after, these same people would be seen eating and laughing together.

This new world intrigued me. Blinded by the illusion of joy and happiness, I wanted badly to be part of what the older kids were experiencing. I began to hang out on the elevator again, pushing floor buttons for folks coming back and forth. I became so well known that I was given the nick-name of Elevator

Boy. Seeing the variety of people ride the elevator impressed me.

Soon, I came to recognize who the working people, the hustlers, pimps, and dope fiends were. The hustlers were the most glamorous. They became my idols. In fact, the only family role model I had was a well-known manager of street women. My uncle, my mother's only brother, was a well-known hustler and pimp whose friends included other "In the game" celebrities such as Ice T., Rudy Ray Moore, Iceberg Slim, and the like. I wanted to be just like him and the other cool guys. I was impressed by their cars, women, the fame, and the money. My road to self-destruction began with this illusion. I was now twelve years old, going on twenty-five.

Though I didn't know it at the time, these illusions helped fill a deep void I had developed. I didn't yet know that I was traumatized. In order to make me feel better about myself, I began to imitate behaviors related to violence, gang-involvement, drinking, drugs, and sex.

Trauma set in as a result of the messages I received from the powerful influences in my life, both familial and societal. At an early age, I was told things like, "You ain't shit and you will never be shit." "You're too black." "You just like your daddy." One of my teachers told me, "You can't be the guy in the picture with the briefcase; you can only be the guy in the picture on the back of the garbage truck." Both my present and future identities were being shaped by these words. As a result of the messages I'd received, and the belief system I'd developed, I set off to find my place in the world.

CHAPTER SEVEN
We Only Know What We Know

Before we begin that journey, let me clear up some myths and/or beliefs about African American families from the improvised communities of America. People of science and religion often refer to these families as dysfunctional or having the inability to integrate into society's mainstream. Although my initial self-description came from the person a child sees as their first teacher, their first love, and their first sense of security, my mother could only pass on the information that had been given to her by her parents, which had been given to her parents by their parents, and so forth until we reached back five or six generations. Their self-development information came directly from the life lived on the slave plantation or some other form of oppression and subjugation.

Many African American parents continued to use the same or similar devices that resembled and caused physical trauma as those found on the plantation. Dr. Joy DeGruy has done extensive research about this topic in her work: *Post Traumatic Slave Syndrome*. Thankfully, over time, not only have I found answers to some of my questions, but I have been able to achieve a higher level of healing.

I couldn't understand why I received such severe beatings from my caregivers, all the while being told that the abuse was because they loved me. Needless to say, I grew up believing that a part of showing love to someone was through the use of physical force.

As I grew up witnessing these things in the Hanover Projects, albeit confusing, my ideas about life were being shaped. After living in foster care where we sang gospel, participated in the recording of a gospel album, and went to church three or four times a week, this new life I was leading was extremely different.

At the time, while in foster care I didn't understand that we were living in the middle class. By the time I was 13, I finally went home for good to live with my mom, and though I was happy to be there, I really began to act out. Because I was basically on my own, I really didn't have the necessary boundaries and structure a teenager needs, and I wasn't restrained from doing a lot of things. Mom worked all day; my brothers and I would generally only see her in the morning and then at nine or ten at night when she picked us up. We were taught not to question why we lived like that. Our grandmother, Big Mama, used to tell us that Mom went to work because she loved us. Once she'd pick us up, we'd go home, fall asleep, wake up, and do the same the next day.

My grandmother drank all the time, so it was really easy to explore many of the things that were forbidden. It was from my grandmother that I stole my first drink of alcohol. I didn't much like the taste and remember getting sick after that first drink. Yet, I continued drinking alcohol as if I was possessed by it. What I liked about it was that it made me feel like I was becoming a man.

CHAPTER EIGHT

Hardly Role Models

As far back as I can remember, I fantasized about comic book heroes and Black exploitation movie characters. I carried around homemade martial arts weapons pretending I was Bruce Lee doing Kung-Fu. Or I copied Dolomite or Superfly by wearing platform shoes and sharkskin suits. I never enjoyed just being myself. After all, I believed I was nobody.

My human role model, at that time, was my Uncle JB, who was a well-known pimp in the city of Rochester; I truly admired what he did, how he did it, and especially how he walked. I admired the girls, the clothes, the big hats, the long shoes, and the different cars. I admired that lifestyle, and wanted to be just like him. It wasn't until much later in life that the illusion was revealed to me. I believed the people around me, who seemed to accept me, were simply a manifestation of my naivety. Much later I found out that the boys I ran with and many of the people that I hung out with whom I considered friends, were not my friends. I remember a time when my boys and I were all walking together as friends, when suddenly two of them jumped me while the other one just stood there and watched. This experience taught me that everyone is not trustworthy.

I recollect being bullied, as many kids are at that age. After being bullied a few times I decided that I would not let it happen to me anymore, and I was no longer going to run. I resolved that I had to win, so I began to act out. I really got the best of anyone I ended up fighting. To protect myself now that my trust in everyone had vanished, I became vicious. I even began to distrust the few people left I could trust.

I continued my escapades, drinking as much as I could. Then my oldest brother, who is about two years older than I am, exposed me to my first use of marijuana. My brother, his friend, and I were in the backyard one day. They were smoking weed and told me that they were going to give me an airplane. This consisted of my brother's friend taking a lit joint into his mouth backwards and blowing smoke into my mouth. Meanwhile, my brother told me to hold the smoke in while he squeezed me from behind until I passed out. This was supposed to represent the ultimate weed high.

My downward spiral continued and my obvious next step was that of participating in gang activity. The gang provided a sense of family, support, and understanding unlike any our parents or other adults could. Our actions included selling drugs, beating people, burglary, and retaliation on other gangs charged with some violation against our gang. Today, we would be known as terrorists but to us, we were just friends who protected each other. We got into a lot of youthful folly.

As time moved on, and as I grappled with differing sets of values and expectations, I acquired some clarity. I realized that what was happening in my life with drug use and gangs was not good for me. Something different needed to happen in my life.–So, at the age of 17, I decided to enlist in the military.

CHAPTER NINE

Trying to Measure Up

Because of my young age, my grandmother had to sign for me to go into the military. I went in with the attitude that I would do things the easiest way possible. I manipulated people and continued stealing and drinking alcohol. I was in the field of Infantry, but felt I'd been lied to because I had been told I was going to be a cook. I have always been interested in cooking. In fact, my grandmother was one of the first black female chefs in the City of Rochester.

As I was saying about my military experience, I went to basic training with the same mode of thinking I'd had in the projects. In other words, wherever I went, I took it with me. During my time in the service, I made some friends, had some challenges, some bouts, and some fights. I continued to drink, which was the one legal drug we could use in the military. I learned ways to get around so that I could drink at the Non-Commissioned Officers' club. I was behaving this way because of my lack of self-esteem, which didn't allow me to measure up to the other soldiers. There was always somebody stronger, faster and somebody this or somebody that.

While I was in Advanced Individual Training, I ended up fracturing my lower back. This gave me a lot of idle time, which caused me to get drunk every day, whether I was on or off campus. Drinking became the main thing I did in life. I had no thoughts about continuing my education nor did I have any other positive goals. I reverted back to familiar behavior. I stole some money and got in trouble. As a result, I ended up getting court martialed. In less than two years, I was back at home, injured, court martialed, and still not understanding the system. Years later I found out I'd gotten a bad conduct discharge which was handed out to me a day before I would have been medically discharged because I was on excess leave. I felt even more powerless and resorted to what I knew best; street life.

In an effort to experience new things and new places, I took a bus all the way back to Rochester rather than a plane. Everywhere the bus stopped, I'd get a drink and a pack of cigarettes. When I arrived home, I continued drinking, smoking cigarettes, and hanging out at bars and clubs all day. Every so often I'd find a job or did some training here or there, but nothing steady.

CHAPTER TEN

Downward Spiral

I came home in May of 1980 around Memorial Day. From that point forward all I did was drink, do drugs and rob people. The resentment I had built up against my mother caused me to steal from her as well. I took from everybody who came into my company: my uncle, my cousin, Teary, everyone. Everyone was a potential victim around me because all I wanted was more. I didn't know anything about the disease of addiction or anything about obsession or compulsion. All I knew was if I wanted something, I had to take it. I stole to support my drinking and getting high, though at the time I didn't know or understand why I was doing it.

Sometime around 1984/1985, I crossed an invisible line. I was introduced to free basing and spent the next 10 years of my life chasing that 1st high. As a result,

I was seduced into a sleepless time warp... When I came to, it was 1994.

Before getting into that realm, I remember people telling me: "You don't want any of that," or, "You don't need to know what they're doing in the basement," and, "Don't touch that, it's not for you." However, I just couldn't wait to try it. I was home!! It became my best friend, my partner, and my comrade. By then, I was mostly a loner. Yet, I never felt lonely as long as I had my drug or the ability to get drugs during the day. My life consisted of living on welfare and trying to get more drugs so I could free base. When I wasn't using drugs, I was drinking until I could get more drugs.

I remember a lot happened between 1988 and 1992. The environment had changed completely with the onset of the crack epidemic. I had been shot on four different occasions, eleven gunshot wounds in total to my body. Most people would have quit or found something different to do after the first shot. One bullet struck me in the head. When it made contact, the bullet managed not to penetrate my skull because it changed directions. One bullet went through my side and two bullets through my hands. About a year later, I was shot again. Every time I was shot, it had something to do with drugs. Yet I still couldn't comprehend that I had a serious problem.

Drugs became everything to me. They gave me the courage to stand up and be vicious, and live for nonexistent virtues over and over again. No matter what happened, I did the same things. Instead of thinking that I might want to stop, I began instead to think I was invincible. It always seemed like I managed to get away with things, or I managed not to be on the scene when others were arrested or got killed.

I did however end up in jail every winter for a few years for stealing or some other activity that supported my habit. Every time I went to jail, I would retreat to religious ideals hoping that would somehow change things. Yet, as soon as I got out, I reverted to the same old habits.

CHAPTER ELEVEN
From User to Dealer

In October 1990, I had the ideal role for a drug addict: drug dealer. I was selling, and had people selling out of my apartment. I got to know a young woman and she and I used together. We always had drugs and it seemed like the perfect situation. However, on October 6, 1990 my girlfriend, who six years later became my first wife, was eight and a half months pregnant. We found ourselves in a situation where drugs came up missing. In the end, I accidentally shot her. I remember being scared beyond belief, but not scared enough to stop and care for my child and its mother. I simply called 911 then ran out the door so I could use the drugs that had been given to me to sell.

It wasn't until three days later, when I was out of drugs, money, and friends, did I begin to think about the shooting. On that third day, I went to the liquor store and got a fifth of Wild Irish

Rose wine. Then I called 911 and waited for the police on the steps of the house where the shooting occurred. As a result of the shooting, our child was still-born, and my girlfriend had lost her dominant arm.

I went to jail for the shooting, and now fully understand the psychological terms of dependence and co-dependence. After about six months of preparing myself to do long, hard time, spewing religion, and praying with anyone who would listen on my cell-block, the charges were dismissed. My girlfriend had refused to press charges. I cried and pleaded that it had happened accidently, and she really felt like it had too. However, this action only resulted in making my self-esteem sink lower and lower because now the worst possible things had happened. My actions resulted in the death of my child and the loss of my girlfriend's arm. I continued to carry that guilt through the first ten years of my recovery. After the incident, my girlfriend and I got back together, and we kept right on using drugs, getting high, and living the same life style. I got shot a couple more times after that. It seemed to be part of the routine until the drugs ran out.

Then the guilt and sorrow would return. I would use more to cover up those feelings. I perceived that what I was engaging in was about power, money, prestige, influence, and hanging out with so-called friends. Though outwardly I appeared and presented like I was indestructible and the "shit." Drugs and money were simply allowing me to hide and medicate a deep self-hatred and sorrow.

CHAPTER TWELVE

The Road to "Rehabilitation"

I was introduced to my first rehabilitation experience in 1991. This came by way of a nudge from a judge, so to speak. I remember being at the center, becoming clean, and presenting as the model patient. I tried all the tricks that people with an active addiction try. Because I believed it wasn't the drugs that were causing my downward spiral, I continued to use. I blamed bad luck and inexperience for my drug use. This whirlwind of self-destruction continued to hurt me and others both emotionally and physically. I kept right on medicating my internal pain and numbing my current existence.

Then, in 1994, at the place we called home (I rarely made it home), I heard a series of gunshots and went out on the porch to see what was going on. I saw this young brother (name withheld) slowly ride by in a car, which was riddled with several bullet holes. It then crashed into a house about five houses down from where I was standing. I rushed towards the car in an attempt to help. It was then that I noticed there was another young man in the passenger seat. He appeared to be dead. I concentrated on the driver. I recognized him as one who frequently walked past the corners where I posted up. Through all the commotion and panic surrounding the scene, my focus was only on the young man I was tending to.

Something happened in my psyche during that pivotal moment. As I was screaming for someone to call an ambulance, the young man said to me, "Help, Help." I tried to reassure him that help was on the way. I noticed that the fire department was first to arrive. A few moments later the police got there. The young man continued to make pleas for help. After what seemed like hours, the ambulance finally arrived. The young man looked me in the eyes with what seemed to be the deepest of concern. I heard him say, "Help" once again, concluding with, "Not me, them!" Then he died.

At that moment my life began to change. I saw my son's face in that young man. I knew I could no longer continue to live like I was. Fortunately, I was able to put my prior experience with rehab and the courts to proper use. Two days after that young man's death, I sought help.

CHAPTER THIRTEEN

The Trap House

Meanwhile, because my addiction and lifestyle were so much a part of who I was, though something had changed within in me after the tragic murder I'd witnessed, I still had a ways to go towards healing. On the evening of August 24th, I set out to go to my usual corner up the street to continue hustling because this is what had become normal to me. On the way, I witnessed the police going to the drug house across the street. The dealer on duty that night ran out of the side door, looked in my direction, then ran towards the back of the house. I had an idea what he was doing: hiding the drugs. I waited while the police were busy with the people inside for my chance to seek out the stash. I went behind the house and found it. There was also a bicycle back there.

I then took the stash and bike and headed to an acquaintance's house then played King of the night trading drugs for sexual favors. I made people act out my fantasies for drugs. The entertainment ended like most other nights: all the drugs and money were gone and I was once again reduced to the role of nobody. The only thing I could think about was how to get more drugs. I could only think of using.

I somehow found my way to another trap house (Place where drugs are used). These people recognized me and let me in. I managed to get $5 from God knows where before I arrived. I used some of what I had, then gave the "house man" his share. Then I came up with a bright idea. I sensed the kid selling drugs in the house was nervous. So, I left the house and went to a pay phone. I called 911 and directed them to the trap house. Then I went back to the house and announced that the police had been called by a user that said she had been beaten by the kid selling drugs. I watched as the kids stashed the drugs then I went behind them, grabbed the stuff, got on the bike, and fled the area towards another part of town. Now I was King for a day once again.

As I began to run low on my supply of drugs that night, for some divine reason I began to think about getting clean so I could be the father, I always desired to be for my son. I also knew that the streets would be hot with dough boys looking for me because of my actions during the last couple of days. My bright idea this time was to escape their retaliation by going back to detox. But I was conflicted because though I wanted to get clean, I also wanted to continue life as I knew it.

The next morning, I used some more then waited for the city transit bus to arrive. I boarded the bus and headed to the community hospital where I knew there was a detox called Day Break. I used my free-base all the way to the door, including on the back of the transit bus. I stashed my drug tools and went in, knowing full well that at some point I was planning to come back out and finish using what drugs I had left.

I was admitted into detox. I attended groups, counseling sessions, and eating and drinking my Ensure. After three days, I had eaten nine meals, taken three or four showers, wore clean underwear and clothes daily, and had three good nights of sleep. I hadn't experienced those simple things and acts of personal care, in many years. I was feeling pretty good about myself both physically and emotionally. Yet, I continued to obsess about what I had stashed outside.

I set out to figure out a way to leave the detox program. I began an argument with someone, don't remember who, and my solution to the argument was to throw a tantrum and leave the detox. As I was making my way towards the exit, I distinctly heard the program counselor known as Betsy W. say, "What's going to be different this time?" I heard her words very clearly and for some reason it affected me profoundly. I didn't let that stop me from going out the door though. However, when I got to the garbage-can ashtray, the cylinder had been emptied, taking my drugs with it. I did the only thing I could think of at the time and went back into the detox center.

I completed the detox program and was shipped off to rehab at St. Jerome's Hospital in Batavia, NY. I was fearful because I began to worry about the unknown. I did not know what my life was going to be like. The rehab guided me through self-discovery and educated me about the disease of addiction. I followed all suggestions from my counselors and completed the program within the allocated 30 days.

When it came time to graduate, I was afraid to go back home. I thought, "I'm not ready yet". As it was, myself and two other patients felt the same way and we decided to take a stand by declaring that we were not going to leave until the social worker found us a halfway house to go to.

Fortunately, our ploy worked. We were held over after our group graduated. The program was unable to find us an empty bed within the next two weeks. Therefore, we were shipped off to Westchester, NY outside NYC to a monastery that served as a homeless shelter and retreat center.

We arrived by bus at St. Christopher's around dinner time. We were invited to eat before being shown our lodging space. We walked into the mess hall and I had never seen so many homeless people in one place at one time. The place was run by monks and the food is what I'd call top-notch; steak, mashed potatoes, and other foods that I can't remember but knew that it was unlike any food I'd eaten at other homeless shelters.

St. Christopher's was situated in the mountains across from West Point

Academy. Every one of us was assigned a job in which we worked 8 hours a day to pay for the 30-day allowed stay at St. Christopher's. It was now the fall of 1994 and early one morning, before I was to start my assigned chores for the day. I got up and went towards the top of a mountain that was near the retreat center.

That morning I witnessed the power and force of the Creator. I saw the fall colors like never before. While I was sitting on top of this mountain, I wrote a poem to my stillborn son Tyrick. I had no idea I could produce such words. Although, somehow the poem has been lost, I can tell you it was an incredibly emotional and apologetic poem. As a result, I actually felt that I would not use again. From that day to this one I have not.

I was finally, truly on my way to recovery at last. Let's make no bones about it, trauma, whether experienced through family discipline practices, social and cultural socialization, generational transmission, or physical and emotional experiences, is real!

I had embarked upon an educational journey of discovery and healing. I read every piece of literature related to trauma that I could get my hands on. I discovered that trauma is defined as: a wound or shock produced by sudden or long-term physical or emotional violence or by an accident. I began to understand the ways in which trauma had impacted my life.

CHAPTER FOURTEEN

Research and Discovery

I found that most theories look into the science of socio-cultural trauma and socialization, and address experiences across ethnic groups throughout the world and over the centuries. I focused however on theories that specifically explore conditions that exist for African Americans. I was most curious about the consequences of multigenerational exposure to oppression, and how it adds to cultural trauma through discipline and socialization practices.

I couldn't help but relate my personal experiences to support the fact that traumatic situations have a damaging effect both in youth and in adulthood. It is difficult to escape years of trauma, especially when engrained in the past, and perceived as the norm. It takes dedication and work to achieve freedom and to escape from the results of it, but it can be done.

Research connecting parenting patterns of African American adults impacted by cultural trauma, and the cultural socialization and discipline practices used to raise their children, appears to be scarce. Most available studies explore the impact of trauma and the connections to socialization of other groups. Therefore, I set out to examine family socialization and African American family discipline practices in particular, and how families socialize their children and the potential impact on later generations.

J. C. Alexander et al. define cultural trauma as: "Something that occurs when members of a collectivity feel they have been subjected to a horrendous event that leaves indelible marks upon their group consciousness, marking their memories forever and changing their future identity in fundamental and irrevocable ways." This type of trauma exists because certain conditions are either inherited or forced upon people by dominating forces. Essentially, it's when a dominant society wants you to believe your existing culture is all wrong and that you need to change your entire belief system. Imagine growing up in a Christian household, for example, then being forced to live in a country where they believe there is no god at all. Any memories and practices you had are forbidden and, furthermore, you are led to believe everything you knew or were taught was all wrong. Imagine the confusion and the longing for the familiar and the deep-rooted anger towards those forcing their culture upon you.

Stamm et al. found that all cultural trauma stems from systems involving colonialism and racism. These systems operate from a foundation in which people of color or of different races and ethnic groups than those in power, are treated as inferior.

People, whether held captive as a prisoner of war or as forced laborers, encounter radical alterations to their character and culture. Alexander et al. and Danieli, DeGruy, Stamm et al. maintain that these systems were designed to force cultural alteration. The oppressed group is left with virtually no choice but to learn how to assimilate into the dominant culture. In other words, the oppressed group is forced to "fit in." Forced to live with strangers at a young age as I was, and forced to adapt to my new family's ideology is an example of such assimilation.

On a much larger scale, after generations of family socialization, the alien culture takes over and becomes seen by the latter generations as its own authentic cultural values. Growing up within an unfamiliar culture, forced me to adapt to ways that I may not have identified with before. I didn't really know who I was because I was adapting to a culture that was not truly mine.

For the African American group, most research on cultural trauma is examined from the point of slavery. Barden's work presents comprehensive reports of scholarship identifying cultural trauma. Among them she identifies "Slavery as the marked traumatic event which helped shape an African American collective identity and memory." Eyerman discovered that everyone in the group suffers injury, as in the case of African Americans, who are a group of people that has achieved some degree of cohesion about the trauma through social movements, familial relationships, and narratives resulting in collective memory."

Several decades ago, scholars within the psychiatric community predicted that people who are victims of trauma may become angry and react compulsively in repeating the trauma. Van der Kolk discusses that trauma can be repeated within the behavioral, emotional, physiologic, and neuro-endocrinological levels of behavior. In addition, experiencing repetition of the trauma on these different levels causes a large variety of individual and social suffering.

Additionally, Van de Kolk discovered that "Anger directed against the self or others is always a central problem in the lives of people who have been violated and this is itself a repetitive re-enactment of real events from the past." This can be seen through my own self-destructive behavior. I not only hurt myself, but many others around me. Being violated by the babysitter at a young age, did more damage than I realized at the time. Though I thought what she was doing was "normal", something didn't sit right with me. The feelings I had about the incident festered until they manifested into anger and guilt. Research suggests that, sexual violations involving boys causes undiagnosed anger and feelings of disgrace that are often expressed through violence or the use of drugs to numb the pain.

Understanding the effects of repeating trauma by inflicting similar trauma on self and others, whether consciously or unconsciously, could be one of the primary sources of what is now referred to as generational trauma. Boyd-Franklin explores and discusses the effects the trauma of slavery as a "cultural process" had on African American families. Furthermore, he suggests that the legacy of slavery impacts the contemporary African American family when parents attempt to socialize their children on how to cope with racism. For example, Akbar, Boyd-Franklin, and DeGruy Leary discovered that when racism is external to a family, it is experienced as discrimination; when racism is internalized, it manifests as a sense of shame about oneself, also known as self-hatred and internalized racism.

One of the ways people overcome such injury is through spirituality. Resilience supported by a deeply entrenched spiritual belief in a better future for their children is one of the greatest strengths and most powerful survival skills of African Americans. According to Boyd-Franklin, sometimes a very deeply ingrained spiritual belief system has sustained families through generations.

African Americans throughout history have put a high value on turning to their faith for assistance. This holds true for the enslaved Africans arriving on the shores of America with various religious beliefs and differing cultural practices, as well as those indoctrinated into Christianity. Joy DeGruy Leary discovered that even in contemporary society, when asked how one made it through a traumatic period, the majority would say it was their faith in God. Furthermore, spirituality to the African American has been a way to address and cope with the psychological. This holds true for the enslaved Africans arriving on the shores of America with various religious beliefs and differing cultural practices, as well as those indoctrinated into Christianity. Furthermore, spirituality to the African American has been a way to address and cope with the psychological pain of racism, because in the African belief system, the psyche and the spirit are one.

Another way that people, particularly children, overcome traumatic injury is when it has taken on a position of normalcy. Gopnik and Wellman discovered, through a series of experiments examining children's use of logic, that a child will fail to accurately report his or her own mental state. The findings further imply that a child will not report on his or her own ideals of what seems natural when what is experienced (whether natural or unnatural) is reinforced by the actions or teachings of others (parents, community, etc.). This would indicate that although the injury exists, a child may not have the capacity to identify the injury due to the perceived normal socialization being practiced by the parenting generation. As depicted in my story, for a long time, I perceived the myriad of events that occurred around me and to me to be normal. I was incapable of expressing that what was happening to me was not normal in any way.

Generational reinforcement of managing the symptoms of trauma by becoming a part of what may be known as a natural function will, at some point, become known as normal behavior. According to Gopnik and Wellman, human beings unlike other species, have unique cognitive capacities to adjust their behavior to what they find out about the world. A long period of protected immaturity, the story might go, plus powerful theory-formation abilities, enable children to learn about the specific cultural and physical features of their world.

Nonetheless, socio-cultural trauma has an impact on socialization, even though humans have the capacity to adjust their behavior to assimilate into their world. The impact of practices used to socialize a child have the ability to remain permanent or unchanged when new knowledge about socializing practices is not available. The enduring oppressive experiences of African Americans have continued to reinforce the impact of cultural trauma. This is in contrast to understanding information that would warrant an adjustment to one's behavior.

In the environment in which I lived, there was no change, there was no learning anything different. And if there was an offering of change, I would not have been able to recognize it because the trauma in my culture was deeply embedded. Even when it was suggested by the judge that I enter rehab, I did it with the same mind frame. I simply went through the motions in order to get back to my old way of life. In my mind, rehab was nothing more than a means to an end.

Several other scholars including Akbar, Crawford et al., Chestang, Hilliard, DeGruy Leary, Poussaint & Alexander have argued that the horrors of slavery were so terrible for so long that, as a result, the trauma was, and continues to be, passed from one generation to the next. Not only are the symptoms of social and cultural trauma very apparent within African American families but also in the general societal framework of America's "melting pot". For example, most ethnic groups and their families in America today have the ability to assimilate into the mainstream, yet this conversion continues to exclude the African American family mostly due to our skin color which clearly identifies us, thus preventing us from blending in.

The historical implications of socio-cultural trauma as previously noted have plagued African American families for countless generations between 1619 and 1865, as well as for the decades that followed. Joy DeGruy points out that many generations were born into the trauma, resulting in the distress itself. This has shaped the memory and identity and has become the people's only known way of life, making it normal to expect agitation and crisis.

CHAPTER FIFTEEN

Impact on Parent Socialization

In the matter of parental socialization, Andrew Meltzoff provides some indications of the learning, memory, and imitation of others by infants as young as 14-18 months of age. This data confirms that even if parents are not intentionally teaching children the mechanisms of urban hassles, inconsistencies, and hostile interactions, infants are capable of preserving these experiences into their memory, which at some point can be assessed and imitated. Alvy, Harris, Bell & Liggins, and Thomas also support these findings. On a personal level, being abandoned by my mother at an early age left me with unconscious memories. When I was left alone in South Carolina crying, hungry and thirsty, I was taught a difficult lesson. Little did I know that I would carry these memories of hurt and anger as I grew up and dealt with others.

Taking into account that not all socialization remains part of our memory, Meltzoff reveals that as a child develops, most learning; whether positive or negative, right or wrong, self-edifying or destructive, remains locked in and is a vital component of a human being's development. Drawing from Hilliards work, there is a recognized need for African Americans to recall and address historical attempts at cultural genocide. Strategies are needed for surviving the cultural losses which are transferred between parent or caregiver and child.

How does one learn social identity, ethnic identity and collective identity? The socialization practices used to instill these aspects of self-worth may not be commonly shared by parents or caregivers. Without intervention or the exploration of *different ways of doing things*, most parents can only raise their children using the same understanding from which they were reared. Programs such as the Effective Black Parenting curriculum are based on the premise that parents can obtain new skills to stop the cycle of misinformation and the continuation of trauma. However, psychological damage suffered can continue to dominate parenting practices, making newly available information of minimal effect on changing family traditions.

According to research focused on ethnic-racial socialization by Hughes, Smith, Stevenson, Rodriguez, Johnson & Spicer, there are four major proposed dimensions of parent socialization:

1. Cultural socialization/ethnic pride
2. Preparation for bias
3. Promotion of mistrust
4. Egalitarianism and silence about race

Cultural socialization/ethnic pride is a process in which admiration of the positive self-concepts of race and culture are taught by parents and caregivers to children. This results in development of racial pride, higher self-esteem, and self-worth. Orellana & Bowman discuss how cultural contexts combine to influence learning and development throughout a child's life while facilitating skills that are used as survival tools within the dominant structural forces. Cultural socialization is also considered a social scientific construct that is central to research focused on parental influences on a child's identity formation.

Hughes, Hughes & Chen suggest that preparation for bias emphasizes a parent's efforts to promote their child's awareness of discrimination and prepares them to cope and navigate through. In studies where open-ended questions were used, results suggest that few parents spontaneously have discussions with their children about discrimination. However, thesee scholars suggest that it is difficult to determine whether the lack of discussion is because preparation for bias is less salient to parents than are other ethnic–racial socialization themes or because discrimination and ethnic–racial biases are too painful or uncomfortable to discuss in the context of interviews with relative strangers.

Hughes et al., discovered that parents do discuss issues related to discrimination with their children, but the frequency varies across ethnic and racial groups. One would think that discussions about racism, bigotry, and bias would be especially common among groups who have historically been oppressed, but some groups rarely discuss these issues with their children.

Another aspect of cultural socialization is the promotion of mistrust. Mistrust born out of the perceived need for suspicion and distrust in interracial interactions. The most prominent practice of promotion of mistrust is preparing the child to mistrust Whites. According to Constantine & Blackmon, messages of racial socialization projecting mistrust may protect urban, black adolescents against some of the harmful effects of a discriminatory environment. Creating a defensive barrier within the societal realm, gives adolescents a sense of security when functioning in an atmosphere that may be unfamiliar to them.

Also, mistrust projects stereotypical messages of socialization as a weapon. Immigrant parents from the West Indies, the Caribbean, and the Dominican Republic, socialize their children to distinguish themselves from native-born African Americans because of African Americans' low social status. Messages of caution and warnings to children about African Americans' stereotypical characteristics are an example of how mistrust is shown within these groups.

Additionally, these messages are also widespread within the native-born African American group itself. According to Hughes et al., this type of mistrust, aimed at protecting children from affiliations with groups who are negatively stereotyped, are different from cautions about closeness to Whites which have been described among African Americans.

This protection of children by establishing suspicion is not only established concerning the white race, it can be seen within the same race. However, this divide is not addressed or discussed as much as the one described with the white race. As a result, this causes a racial divide within the same race and different and confusing messages are received by the youth.

Another aspect is egalitarianism (fairness) and being silent about race. When a parent or caregiver fails to mention racial issues, it communicates race-related values and views among children. Hughes et al., suggest that many parents socialize their children to either value individual people's qualities over race, or these parents simply avoid discussions of race with their children altogether. This socialization practice called "mainstream socialization" suggests that rather than parents orienting their children toward their native minority status, culture, and heritage, they focus on developing skills and characteristics needed to assimilate into the mainstream, or dominant, culture.

Living with strangers forced me to develop skills in order to blend in to their environment. I may not have chosen to be a gospel singer or belong to a singing group. This was a culture that was not truly mine, but one I had to mirror in order to survive in an alien society. I developed coping skills rather than an identity in which to grow into instead of having to escape from it later in life.

Hughes et al., show that parents most commonly mentioned cultural socialization and equal opportunity as important. Messages concerning racial pride and appreciating diversity are most central to parents' child-rearing. However, the majority of minority parents report that they prepare their children for bias as well, especially

African American parents, who are the most likely to report preparation for bias.

There was no discussion about race within my family, so I was left unaware and unprepared for societal bias. It was left up to my interpretation, which was one without example.

It is argued by Stamm, Stamm IV, and Hudnail & Higson-Smith that a parent's traumatic stress may carry forward to the next generation because of the parent's impaired ability to parent. It may also be transmitted through a shared belief system that is held by the parent, the family, or even the culture. Types of socialization, particularly racial socialization, vary depending on the amount of emotion and resources that the parent has available. White-Johnson, Ford & Sellers found that parents who are older may have more life experiences with the meaning and implications of race than younger parents. How meaning is made of experiences is influenced by how trauma has impacted the family over generations. Without knowledge of how earlier generations have been impacted, current families continue to socialize in ways that could continue the negative impact of the trauma.

For me, I had no prior knowledge of how my family was impacted by societal bias. As a result, I functioned by watching what strangers did and how the people in the projects functioned. These were my examples. By me not knowing how to live in this type of society, I was perpetuating the cycle of trauma. I dealt drugs, was violent, and lived in a way that I guessed was the right path.

Families often socialize their children based on the methods shown to them or learned from their own family. In my case, I was not taught anything about this topic. I had no family examples to reference. My only point of reference came from living in a home with strangers. I did not learn anything about this matter from my mother since we had only brief encounters at the local restaurant. I had to adapt without guidance. I didn't know the "rules" related to socializing.

Although families from different cultural backgrounds may have different socialization goals for their children, Li, Costanzo & Putallaz discovered that families socialize their children according to the cultural values and norms of their particular cultures. Socialization can also be viewed in relation to others. One's identity or self is entangled with many others. The inner circle of a person affects their identity. How someone acts and reacts can be traced back to the people with whom they surround themselves. The most significant inner circle member is the parent. The self is constructed in part from the socialization practices of the parent. The parent is the main source as relates to how children learn their behavior. This cycle gets repeated across generations.

My construction, my actual being was puzzled together by a myriad of people who were not my family. I learned unconscious behaviors from the babysitter, the drug dealers, the pimps, the junkies, and the locals for whom I pushed buttons on the elevators in the projects. These people were my "significant others." What I heard and saw became my truth and built how I would see myself and the world.

CHAPTER SIXTEEN

Impact on the African American Family

Society maintains a set of perceptions and stereotypes. Society makes assumptions about African American people's character and the concept of race. Loury discusses the fact that this negative perception about African Americans is determined without any consideration given to the possible lasting effects of trauma that have and continue to occur throughout the psyche of its members.

Some scholars suggest that African Americans suffer a pariah status. This status stems from the denial that the problem pertains to race. Stereotyping, social isolation, cultural styles all hinder understanding by others. The absence of community assistance and guidance deters education for African Americans. Without educating internally and externally, the cycle will remain unchanged. African Americans will continue to be outcasts in a society that only knows typecasts. In order to gain comprehension, the plight of African Americans and their history needs to be known. If this does not occur, races will continue to remain separate.

An ever-widening rift concerning the importance of race in contemporary America still exists. African Americans see race as important while most other races think African Americans are obsessed with race. This rift deters unification across racial lines, such as efforts to solve commonly shared local matters. The ideal of Blacks and Whites living together in universal brotherhood through integration has never achieved broad appeal due to this rift.

African Americans being obsessed with race causes continued division while overlooking the significance of the distress that has been impressed on a people. The natural continuum of human development has been traded in for mirrored glasses, making the victim the perpetrator. Remembering and forgetting are two sides of the same phenomenon: the past in the present. People also defend themselves from painful memories by blocking out the agony. The memory is there at some level, but people do their best to avoid it. Sometimes the memory is taken in and transformed, and in that state, remains in the back of the mind but not as the original experience.

The fact that painful memories are still present but not necessarily recognized, helps us understand the relationship between violent behavior and the cultural value system of African Americans. A relationship exists between a traumatized adult and the learned self-concept of their children.

Characteristics of how people interact with the world around them include:

1. Axiology

2. Epistemology

3. Logic

4. Process

The assumptions that these characteristics produce are almost never questioned.

Axiology, the study of the nature and criteria of values for specific cultural groups, determines how a group adapts over time. This adaptation determines the value system of the group and will be the model for future generations to follow.

According to Nichols, Member-Member is the primary value system of African Americans. This indicates that the highest value is placed on the "relationship" between individuals. The relationship is the most important factor in regulating the majority of human activities within the culture. The survival of the group is primarily dependent upon the integrity of relationships among the members of that group.

As previously stated, my relationships with my family and others were always ones of not belonging and not knowing. The way I decided to belong was to act out in a negative manner. My survival depended on my interpretation of the cultural group, or who I perceived to be family. Not knowing the history and background about my family, created a disadvantage for me and only contributed to the trauma that was hidden within my subconscious. I was reacting on the basis of memories that I didn't realize existed.

Differences in cultural situations that impact families and shape the development of minority and mainstream children were not considered when studying minority children and families. African Americans socialize their children as a means of survival in the American social construct. The child internalizes the behavior of development as a normal process, and then socializes their own children in the same manner.

Despite the attributes of strength and resilience in African American families, it still remains challenging to develop in a positive way and achieve success while still functioning with unresolved cultural trauma. African American experiences of chattel slavery have continued to impact generations of families up until the present.

Studies suggest that because of enslavement over generations, many African Americans have internalized anxiety or harbor feelings of inadequacy. They do not feel valued in society. This leads to a low sense of self-worth and identity issues. These messages are inherited and engrained through generations.

Socialization of children in an environment that consists of urban hassles, inconsistencies, and hostility, also contributes to ideals of family structures as well as individual and collective self-concepts. In using what is referenced as the Traditional Black Discipline of children as an example, Alvy, Harris, Bell & Liggins, discuss that during slavery, parents tended to apply harsh, often aggressive, discipline on children as a survival tactic. The purpose was to keep their children out of harm's way or prevent them from being disciplined by the master, the overseer, or someone else in authority. Parents may have also used this harsh discipline to look powerful to their children and hide the fact that they were powerless.

In my experiences, I endured harsh parental practices and inconsistencies. As told, my mother left me as a child alone in a house in South Carolina. Unknowingly, I had to cope with this situation and take care of myself. Also, I learned to rely on myself in her absence. When I did finally spend time with my mom, it was a brief meeting at a local restaurant. During this time, my focus was more on pleasing her and not making her angry or disappointed with me. As I got older and went back to live with her, she was never home. She worked a lot so I had the freedom to do whatever I wanted. There wasn't any consistency in my household.

Though neither my mother or grandmother inflicted physical harm on me, my mother put me in an environment where I had to endure harsh beatings from "surrogate parents." To show their power over me, they would physically harm me when they were not pleased by my singing, behavior, and my forgetfulness of gospel passages. They molded me into what they thought I should be as a young African American male. Not realizing that this fear they created in me only showed me that to get what I want I must instill pain and terror. Perhaps my mother thought she was protecting me by placing me in such a cruel setting rather than keeping me with her at the projects. This is one major practice of socialization in which the trauma is unconsciously reinforced in its transmission through child discipline practices.

Another example of unconscious reinforcement is found in the book, *That Mean Old Yesterday*. In an excerpt the author explains how a slave mother justifies her actions of abusing her child with a variety of instruments. The parent defends her actions by saying if she didn't implement the abuse, then the white slave owner would. This can be seen as taking the control away from the slave owner and putting it back into the hands of the parent so she can protect her own child.

Ultimately the child is socialized to continue the behavior on to the next generation due to learning the behavior on the social level (the family) and then on the individual level (internalizing the learned behavior). This behavior mirrors Vygotsky's social development theory.

Thomas evaluated Kerby T Alvy's 1990 Effective Black Parenting program. In his work he concurs with prior research concerning the parental socialization of African American children resulting from the traumatic experience of slavery and continuing after the physical end of that atrocity. Traditional discipline among African Americans was inconsistent, harsh and had irrational standards. Black parents continued to discipline this way because it was the customary way stemming from the traumatic history of slavery. There is a need for African American parents to develop a practical replacement for traditional discipline. Replacing the disciplinary practices of old would help break the cycle of harsh punishments learned during the traumas of slavery.

To summarize, although it's been several decades since the signing of the Civil Rights Act and America has been dubbed by some as a post-racial society, the residuals of slavery, Jim Crow Laws, and the legacy of racism have left an impact on the psyche of the African American. This is depicted in today's society where cultural trauma and its history still exist. The trauma continues to impact the African American family and family socialization.

Although modern thought is that America is a much more racially open-minded society, the results of past events have influenced the socialization practices that African Americans tend to continue on a foundation of caution and apprehension. As indicated by Dr. Joy DeGruy, conditions that have persisted include: learned helplessness, literacy deprivation, distorted self-concept, antipathy or aversion to members of one's own identified cultural/ethnic group, including physical characteristics or mores and customs. The collective memory of these traumas has often dictated peoples' cultural and socialization practices. African American children will continue to learn from the adults in their lives what it means to be African American and how to endure the invisible societal norms that perpetuate the cultural trauma.

Cultural trauma has an impact on the contemporary parental socialization processes without any actual or cognitive parental connection to the transmitted injury. Also, the limited research available connecting the parenting patterns of African American adults impacted by trauma and the cultural socialization or practices used to raise their children has left little in-depth reference regarding the injuries impacting this group. Examining the possible relationship between cultural socialization and discipline practices as a specific form of parental socialization, allows for some understanding. To achieve more understanding, one has to focus on ethnic pride and preparation for bias as forms of parental socialization, and the impact of discipline practices to represent the generational influences related to cultural trauma.

CHAPTER SEVENTEEN

Exploring Cultural Trauma

Exploring cultural trauma is important in understanding its relationship to cultural socialization practices in African American families. When examining cultural socialization practices, one should take into account how it filters and influences generations. Many African American families are using historically accepted parental socialization methods, adapted from generations who experienced traumatic social conditions.

These methods of socialization are outdated in the sense that though the strategies potentially served a historical purpose, they have not been reexamined, resulting practices seen as supported by the culture. African Americans are impacted by cultural trauma and the practices used to socialize children within families are often a result of that trauma.

I have been researching this topic for a very long time. The data I collected for my personal research was conducted during a conference sponsored by Ujima Rochester, Inc., which had a focus on *healing from cultural trauma: A Time for Healing, Educating, and Rebuilding III: Exploring Socio-Cultural Trauma 150 Years after Emancipation, Embracing Solutions.* This was a training and professional development conference, which is an annual Ujima Rochester, Inc. event catered mainly to human service and education professionals. However, the conference was also open to interested members of the general public as it was widely advertised on radio, through emails to professional service organizations, local school districts, and a range of regional colleges and universities.

The conference took place at a local downtown hotel conference center in Rochester, NY, an inner-city with approximately 210,000 residents. African Americans make up nearly half (42%) of

Rochester's population with almost 32% of them living in poverty. At the time, the high school graduation rates for African American males in the city school district ranged between 27 and 34 percent.

Some important information about Ujima Rochester, Inc.; It addresses racial and cultural disparities by offering pro-social development services for youth and families, social justice consulting, Afrocentric education, and emergency service referrals for runaway/ homeless youth. The organization's mission is to provide integrated and multidisciplinary services that respond to the needs of youth and their families through intensive and quality programs that promote pro-social behavior and contribute to public safety.

This conference provided an opportunity to get more information about cultural trauma that could be beneficial to the African American community. The lack of education surrounding this topic was something I previously mentioned as needed to change the way African Americans think and react in regards to discipline and socialization.

Over the course of the two-day conference, I was able to hear the keynote describe Post Traumatoc Slave Syndrome and heard a presentation on The Effects of Socio-Cultural Trauma in the Urban Church. In addition, the conference offered breakout sessions where participants could attend up to eight different sessions. The breakout sessions addressed various topics for individuals, families, and communities related to cultural trauma: Finding Solutions to Healing from Generations of Socio-Cultural Trauma (panel discussion); The Importance of Respect for African American & Urban Youth; Mental Illness in The Black Community; Socio-Cultural Trauma and its effects within (a) Latino Culture, (b) Latino Church, and (c) Native American Culture; African American experiences of witnessed Intimate Partner Violence (IPV) and Clinical

Implications; Socio-Cultural Trauma in the African American Community, and Trauma and the State of Contemporary Youth in Rochester.

Participants

I collected 132 completed surveys for my data. Although my research focused mainly on African American parent socialization, neither race nor ethnicity was a criterion for completing the survey. Individuals were eligible to be included in analyses for the research study if they had: registered as a participant in the educational conference, self-identified as African American, and were over the age of eighteen.

Once I gathered the data, I determined a number of participants in the survey that I could test further allowing me to divide the information into distinct groups exclusively focusing on African American adults. I conducted additional research and analysis as I'd discovered there is a lack of research on the relationship with discipline practices and cultural socialization.

I focused on two significant research questions regarding discipline practices and cultural socialization in African American families. I defined cultural socialization as a multidimensional, multigenerational construct which includes the socialization of African American cultural values, intracultural interactions, cultural embeddedness, African American history and heritage, and the promotion of ethnic pride. In addition, it includes teaching about racial barriers and living and coping with racism. Part of the study is based on my previous research which showed that much of the socio-cultural trauma affecting urban communities of America is the result of lingering generational behaviors and present-day experiences related to socialization practices.

When I examined the perspectives of different generations, the data revealed the impact of trauma, how it has polluted multiple generations and led to repeated patterns within the family. This may help explain certain behavioral patterns, symptoms, roles, and values adopted by family members, family sources of vulnerability as well as resilience and strength, and job choices (following in the footsteps of a relative, a namesake) through the generations. When I view this from a family systems perspective, what happened in one generation will affect what happens in the older or younger generation, though the actual behavior may take on a variety of forms.

Socialization and Discipline Practices

All families socialize their children to help them learn and understand how to function within the society in which they live. Through my research I found that for African American families, these processes involve teaching their children how to function in a society in which they will experience racism. Given the history of racism in the United States, parents or caregivers' own socializing experiences as a child will impact what is considered important to address in socializing the next generation. Corporal discipline has historically been used to ensure obedience, and among African Americans, was explicitly used for this purpose by slave owners. According to Joy DeGruy and others, it continued to be a pattern of disciplining to teach children compliance at home in order to encourage obedience with "knowing your place" in a society where the discipline associated with non-compliance could result in death. I discovered however, that research examining the relationship between socialization and discipline practices among African Americans was lacking. Because of this, I sought to examine these relationships among individuals attending the conference, which focused on healing from the impact of historical racist practices that have negatively influenced current experiences.

When I examined what the keynote said, I found consistent

references to history and contemporary experiences, reflecting on the conference which had a focus on the need for group healing. The information could be used on a personal level however, the broader concept was to become aware of historical patterns that have left groups of people (i.e., African Americans, Latinos, and Native Americans) wounded and in need of healing. The healing, while it may be different for each group, can only be interpreted by the individuals themselves.

I discovered a strong relationship between the current practices of verbal discipline and current practices of physical discipline in the African American family. There was a strong positive relationship between current practices of verbal discipline and restrictive discipline (time out and privileges taken). The current practices I reported on included verbal discipline with the use of either physical discipline or restrictive discipline. In contrast, experiencing physical discipline as a child showed a significant negative relationship with both verbal and restrictive disciplines. When physical discipline was used during one's childhood, verbal or restrictive discipline was generally not used.

When I looked at the overall model for discipline received as a child, there was no difference across forms of discipline received. Within the model, however, the impact of discipline across types of punishment experienced and the current age of participants (i.e., physical, verbal, and restrictions) showed a statistical trend. What I found suggests that older participants, many who potentially had socializing roles, may have developed an appreciation for the discipline they received as a child due to these individuals reporting a higher level of harsh discipline that was also related to practices still in use. When there is a significant relationship lacking with cultural socialization, there is a possible disconnect between discipline and socialization practices that instill racial pride and prepares for encounters of racial bias. While discipline is a socializing practice, I found that the practices experienced were not related to being prepared for racial bias as an African American.

This "disconnect" raises concerns for me about the continued use of discipline practices that have little relevance in preparing African American children and youth for contemporary experiences of racism. I discovered that although the number of participants that reported experiencing physical discipline as a child was lower among younger than older individuals, they still reported it as a current discipline practice that remained impactful. Physical punishment continues to be used and potentially has a continued negative impact. However, its use is not understood as being connected to enduring racialized experiences. When I explored these practices, I was able to find statistical relationships, but there was limited information in regards to the interpretation of these numbers. A future study could be utilized to explore how these practices were shaped and influenced by history.

Discipline Practices by Age

In order to understand the impact of age, I conducted an additional ANOVA test examining age on participants' ratings of cultural socialization, preparation for bias, and cultural pride. I found there was significance for cultural pride but not for preparation for bias. There were differences across age that exist for having been socialized on cultural pride but not on preparation for bias: older participants were different from younger participants on cultural pride. However, I discovered that the lack of a significant finding related to preparation for bias suggests that across each age group, there may be some socialization taking place in addressing bias so differences across ages were not found.

Given the setting at the conference where the data was collected, I thought another interpretation was worth considering: The exposure to new historical information. It is difficult to know whether participants would have considered being prepared for bias while growing up if they were not comparing that knowledge to the historical content they received at the conference. The keynote address, in addition to some breakout sessions, presented racism and racial bias on multiple levels from the individual level to the systemic, structural level. The content of the presentation provided details about how racism is maintained and how that has impacted the humanity of African American families and children. It appears that participants who believed they had been prepared for dealing with bias, learned during the conference that the bias was more extensive than previously thought. This may have contributed to a shift in believing one had not been adequately prepared after all.

This leads us back to my personal account of the impact of trauma and its effect on self-worth, self-love, family, and community relationships, collective and victorious thought, and the impulse to live a life wrought with illusion and recurring destructive patterns.

CHAPTER EIGHTEEN

On the Journey Towards Healing

Watching a young man die right in my arms, his identity mistaken, changed me. To this day, I don't know what happened internally or even spirituality. I didn't see a burning bush or a bolt of lightning. By this time, I had a second child, besides the one who had died. I knew I had to do something differently if I wanted what I always dreamed of, to be a father, to be a dad. Though I didn't have any good examples of what a father should be like, I badly wanted to be a good father myself.

I was fortunate enough to go to a detox center, rehab, and through the cycle of substance abuse treatment. That was twenty-five years ago. It was not until around 2004 that I began to understand that all the terrible things I'd done were not reflective of my true self, but rather were committed by the guy who was addicted to drugs.

Twenty-five years later I am still clean from drugs and I've learned many valuable lessons during this time. My ideas of what a good father is challenged everything I thought I knew about being a dad. I needed to take care of my son, and I needed to care for my child's mother. I really don't know what convinced me to take care of him. It could have been the shame and guilt I felt, or it could have been the mere realization that he is my child, my responsibility.

This began a period of realization for me in terms of what life is all about. Though I'd experienced an awful lot during my life, I was undeveloped in living life as so-called "normal people" do, because of my lack of knowledge. I wasn't one of those recovering addicts who had lost a wife, a home, and a good job. Instead, I had no education and had never worked a job for any significant period of time. I had never owned a car and I never really owned anything. My only "home" consisted of apartments through welfare when I was actively using drugs. Basically,

I was out there trying to learn how to live life on my own without much direction. I didn't realize that everything I knew about living was distorted. I didn't understand I was suffering from cultural trauma or social trauma or trauma period. Trauma sounded like something big and scary and, of course, I didn't think I was anguishing from it. Nevertheless, it was real and it affected me in all areas of my life and in all the decisions I made. Back when I was in foster care, I didn't know that there weren't any fathers around my other brothers too. At that age, I considered I was the only victim of abandonment. All I knew was that I was constantly being left and didn't understand why.

Another thing I didn't understand was what my mother was going through herself. None of these things made sense, so most of my life I felt abandoned and did certain things and behaved in certain ways in order to protect myself. I sabotaged relationships as soon as they began because I felt they were going to end anyway. I did this so I wouldn't get hurt. Also, I would be inconsiderate and overly aggressive in order to protect what I had learned to survive in the streets.

Although I was negatively impacted by these occurrences, I learned some valuable lessons. I became keenly aware of my surroundings at all times. If I feel any kind of way that doesn't seem comfortable or doesn't feel just right, I've learned to follow that instinct. I've been saved by that feeling numerous times.

Additionally, I've learned that I'm not alone in my suffering, for which there isn't a diagnosis because there is no cure. I'm not the only one who suffers like this or has been through this level of suffering.

Since I've been clean and serene, my eyes have been opened wide and I have learned a lot over the years. The difference is that I am now allowing these learnings to take place. I am relearning how to live and am open to it. No more self-sabotage and destroying my emotional well-being. No longer will phrases like, "you ain't shit," "you ain't gonna be shit," "you're stupid" or "you're too black," be projected onto me. No one is telling me this kind of nonsense anymore and even if these words were said, I would no longer hear them, nor would I internalize them.

Though I have been making gains, there are still parts of me struggling through the unconscious trauma. Trauma perpetuates emotional instability. At times I still perceive myself as unworthy. I have a tendency towards anger. These feelings are self-induced, and it has been very difficult to overcome them. It is challenging to fight these feelings when I am not sure where their roots are anchored.

However, even with these obstacles, I am now living in my recovery, have gained a formal education, and have become culturally centered into understanding that I am so much more than I ever knew.

Plenty has happened in my life. Much too much to fit into one book. Several volumes with more precise details would be necessary. This book is a labyrinth where the different paths and walls represent the chapters of my experiences. At times I still wrestle with the direction of my journey.

In my almost 26 years of recovery, I have been married twice. I became a father, and had the opportunity to break the cycle within my family where my children are concerned. I fought for and gained custody of them. I have been able to help numerous people find recovery and numerous children find themselves.

I continue to work with gang members and those children who are the hardest to serve. I realize that life is going to be difficult at times. I have great, happy times, yet every so often life throws me a test. But I haven't found it necessary to return to my old life; in fact, I've been able to live two lives in one lifetime. Most of the things I have learned, people are dying to experience.

I hope that my story will inspire future generations. As I continue my research into socialization by parents who are impacted by cultural trauma, I hope to further guide those who seek to help children, teach children, and be role models for children. I want to be a part of breaking the cycle in many children's lives. In spite of all those things I learned to believe about myself in the past, I've been so blessed. I never knew that one day I would be doing the things I am now doing and be in the position that I am in.

To understand cultural trauma, there must be enlightenment. My hope is that more people not only listen but apply what they learn about cultural trauma from my experiences and my research. When this happens, the cycle can be broken and growth can occur.

There remain many preconceived notions and myths about the African American family. I don't cater to the idea that families are dysfunctional. I believe our parents gave us the best they could with what they had. I now understand that discipline practices were carried over from the plantation and were often used to socialize African American children. Yes, tragedies, traumas, and cultural trauma happened in other cultures as well, particularly to the Jews, the Native Americans, the Asian Americans, and the Latino Americans. However, I am primarily focused on the African American.

As Harriet Tubman once stated: "If I could've convinced more of my people that they were slaves, I could have freed more of them." If similar scholars and I could convince more folks that there is something deeply rooted in our psyche that impacts our children as well as adult development, then I would be able to help more people. However, I understand that all I can do is plant the seeds, water them as often as they will allow me to water them, and allow them to grow.

I never dreamed that I would be able to achieve the learning I've attained. I am now a community advocate, and work in a community where people are glad to see me coming, rather than locking their doors, hiding their purses or waiting for the unexpected.

I am able to do so many things and had so many people who influenced me along the way: Dr. Raymond Graves, and Dr. Olive Akosua, whom has passed on now. People whom I didn't know very well; Dr. Asa Hillard, Dr. John Henry Clark; Dr. Ben Johanen. My friends Tood Williams; Impenda Sara; Jimmy Addison; Brother Simba; Betsy Wilson, just so many people who have given me gifts and passed them on to me and are no longer here. I am so fortunate that I was able to reveal to my mother and my grandmother whom I have become, to have them proud of me, and want me in their company.

For the reader, I do not intend to give you the impression that transformation and healing is easy, yet I guarantee it's worth it! Healing begins with a desire to do or be someone different than your current self. One's mind and heart must be open to receiving new information. Especially, when it contradicts the information that was given as part of your socialization. I will also say that this is not the time, nor is it appropriate, to use the journey towards healing as an excuse to blame or criticize those that taught you what they knew. It is important to lace your foundation of healing with the understanding that your parents or guardians did the best they could with the information they had.

As you and hopefully those you love, move towards healing and transformation there are some suggestions. Dr. Joy DeGruy in her work *Post Traumatic Slave Syndrome*, outlines seven steps towards healing. These suggestions or steps are relatively universal and are extremely helpful towards recovery and beyond. I am in agreement that these steps are of great help and I highly recommend following them.

The foundation of health is telling the truth; truth about family history, the societal experience, and questionable things that have become the norm. Build upon your strengths, the ones you were born with as well as what you have learned from others. Monitor and manage stress and conflict, stress is a silent killer. Learn about racial socialization and how to prepare yourself, your family, and those in your circle to be culturally prepared for the future. Take a look at the person in the mirror. Are you satisfied with who you have become and are you open to working towards change? Be sure to build esteem and uplift all those you come in contact with. In other words, along your journey, be the healing that you seek.

These are just a few of the things you should keep in your toolbox. Please be aware that healing doesn't happen overnight, there is no medication that you can take for it and there is no instant fix. It is a journey, and just when you think you've reached the highest point in your healing, you may want to check again. Because as long as society or individuals continue to hit you where you were previously injured, the healing process may slow down.

Surprising yet true, while you are on your path to healing you may encounter resistance from those closest to you. Especially family members, spouses, and friends. In my experience moving towards healing can be a lonely road. Simply because the information you have gathered and learned along your journey remains new to others. Therefore, it is not wise to expect all of our loved ones to understand or relate to how far we've come nor where we are during the healing process.

I suggest that if you know someone who is having a difficult time with your new lease on life, try thinking outside the box in order to share information. For example, maybe share a book with them on the subject, or purchase an e-book as a gift, or maybe invite them to watch a movie produced by one of many scholars on the subject.

Now that you have reached the end of this book, pass it on to someone you believe it may help. Ase.' I pray that you're able to relate and move towards healing. Surround yourself with those who can support you and encourage you along the way. My healing was not achieved on an individual level, it has always been a collective journey and the value of the "village" should not be underestimated nor ignored.

I'd like everyone both young and old, to understand, that no matter what situation or circumstance you're facing; hope is tangible, hope is achievable, hope can be obtained. We get an opportunity if we're willing to do the work to change our lives beyond our wildest dreams. I am a product of all that could be detrimental, dangerous, and painful, but have managed to come through it all, get to the other side, and find my life's purpose. Yes, it's been a struggle, but it's one that I wouldn't give up for the world. Today I am somebody, I am worthwhile, I matter...

BIBLIOGRAPHY

Abrudan, F. (2011). *Cultural trauma and Africa diaspora*. Retrieved from Academia.edu: *www.academia.edu/1156261/Cultural_Tr auma*

Akbar, N. (1996). *Breaking the chains of psychological slavery*. Tallahassee, FL: Mind Productions.

Alexander, J. C., Eyerman, R., Giesen, B., Smelser, N. J., & Sztompka, P. (2004). *Cultural Trauma and Collective Identity.* Berkeley, CA: University of California Press.

Alexander, M. (2012). *The New Jim Crow: Mass incarceration in the age of colorblindness.* New York, NY: The New Press.

Andersen, S. M., & Chen, S. (2002). *The relational self: An interpersonal social-cognitive theory*. Psychological Review, 109(4), 619-645.

Asante, M. K. (1991). *The Afrocentric idea in education.* Journal of Negro Education, 170-180.

Assel, M. A., Landry, S. H., Swank, P. R., Steelman, L., Miller-Loncar, C., & Smith, K. E. (2002). How do mothers' childrearing histories, stress and parenting affect children's behavioral outcomes? Child: Care, Health & Development, 28(5), 359–368.

Barden, K. P. (2013). Remembering the cultural trauma legacies of slavery: African American young adult perceptions on racism, ethnic identity, and racial socialization (Doctoral dissertation). Available from ProQuest Dissertations and Theses database. (UMI No. 3596996)

Baumrind, D. (2005). Patterns of parental authority. Special Issue: Changing boundaries of parental authority during adolescence. New Directions for Child and Adolescent Development, 108, 61–69.

Bell, C. (1994, September). Finding a way through the maze of racism. Emerge, 5(11), 80.

Boyd-Franklin, N. (2003). *Black families in therapy: Understanding the African American experience.* (2nd ed.). New York: Guilford Press.

Boykin, A. W., & Toms, F. D. (1985). *Black child socialization: A conceptual framework.* In H. P. McAdoo, & J. L. McAdoo (Eds.), Black children: Social, educational and parent environments. Newbury Park, CA: Sage.

Brave Heart, M. (2001). Historical trauma response. The Circle News, Native American News and Arts, 22.

Brave Heart, M., & Debruyn, L. M. (1998). The American Indian holocaust: Healing historical unresolved grief. American Indian and Alaska Native Mental Health Research, 8(2), 56.

Brown, T. L., & Krishnakumar, A. (2007). Development and validation of the Adolescent Racial and Ethnic Socialization Scale (ARESS) in African American families. Youth Development, (36), 1072-1085.

Bryant, W. W. (2011). Internalized racism's association with African American male youth's propensity for violence. Journal of Black Studies, 42(4), 690-707.

Chestang, L. W. (1972). Character development in a hostile environment (Occasional Paper). Chicago, Illinois: University of Chicago.

Cohen, J. (1988). *Statistical power analysis for the behavioral sciences.* Hillsdale, NJ: Lawrence Erlbaum Associates.

Committee for Children. (2016). Powerful parenting: Building relationships and instilling confidence. Retrieved from http://www.cfchildren.org/second-step/social-emotional-learning/powerful-parenting

Constantine, M. G., & Blackmon, S. M. (2002). Black adolescents' racial socialization experiences: Their relations to home, school, and peer self-esteem. Journal of Black Studies, 32(3), 322-335.

Crawford, J., Nobles, W. W., & Leary, J. D. (2003). *Reparations and health care for African Americans: Repairing the damage from the legacy of slavery.* In R. Winbush (Ed.), Should America pay? Slavery and the raging debate on reparations. (pp. 251-281). New York: Harper Collins Publishers.

Danieli, Y. (1998). *International handbook of multigenerational legacies of trauma.* New York: Plenum Press.

DeGruy Leary, J. (2005). *Post Traumatic Slave Syndrome: America's legacy of enduring injury and healing.* Milwaukie, OR: Uptone Press.

Dodge, K. A., McLoyd, V. C., & Lansford, J. E. (2005). *The cultural context of physically disciplining children.* In V.C. McLoyd, N.E. Hill, & K.A. Dodge (Eds.), African American family life: Ecological and cultural diversity. Duke Series in Child Development and Public Policy (pp. 245-263). New York, NY: Guilford Press.

Elmore, C. A., & Gaylord-Harden, N. (2013). The influence of supportive parenting and racial socialization messages on African American youth behavioral outcomes. Journal of Child and Family Studies, 22(1), 63-75.

Evans-Campbell, T. (2008). Historical trauma in American Indian/Native Alaska communities: A multilevel framework for exploring impacts on individuals, families, and communities. Journal of Interpersonal Violence, 23(3), 316-338.

Eyerman, R. (2001). *Cultural trauma: Slavery and the formation of African American identity.* New York, NY: Cambridge University Press.

Fuller, N. (1964). The united-independent compensatory code/system/concept: A textbook/workbook for thought, speech, and/or action, for victims of *racism (white Supremacy). CR Publishers.

Gershoff, E. T. (2002). Corporal punishment by parents and associated Child behaviors and experiences: A meta-analytic and theoretical review, Psychological Bulletin, 128(4), 539-579.

Harrison, A. O., Wilson, M., Pine, C. J., Chan, S., & Buriel, R. (1990). Family ecologies of ethnic minority children. Child Development, 61, 347-367.

Heru , A. M. (2013). Families in psychiatry: Preventing the transmission of trauma. Clinical Psychiatry News, 41(3), 9.

Hill, R. B. (2003). The strengths of Black families. Lanham, MD: University Press of America.

Hilliard, A. G. (1997). SBA: *The reawakening of the African mind.* Gainesville, Florida: Makare Publishing.

Hines, P. M., & Boyd-Franklin, N. (2005). African American families. Ethnicity and Family Therapy, 3, 87-100.

Hofstede, G. (1997). *Cultures and organizations: Software of the mind.* New York: McGraw Hill.

Hughes, D., & Chen, L. (1997). When and what parents tell children about race: An examination of race-related socialization among African American families. Applied Developmental Science, 1(4), 200-214.

Hughes, D., & Johnson, D. (2001). Correlates in children's experiences of parents' racial socialization behaviors. Journal of Marriage and Family, 63(4), 981–995.

Hughes, D., Smith, E. P., Stevenson, H. C., Rodriguez, J., Johnson, D. J., & Spicer, P. (2006). Parents' ethnic-racial socialization practices: A review of research and directions for future study. Developmental Psychology, 42(5), 747-770.

Johnson, L.B., & Staples, R. (2002). *Black families at the crossroads: Challenges and prospects.* Hoboken, NJ: John Wiley & Sons.

Karenga, M. (1986). Social ethics and the Black family: An alternative analysis. The Black Scholar, 41-54.

Kellermann, N. P. (2013). Epigenetic transmission of Holocaust Trauma: Can nightmares be inherited? Israel Journal of Psychiatry and Related Sciences, 50(1).

Kellermann, N. P. (2001). Perceived parental rearing behavior in children of Holocaust survivors. Israel Journal of Psychiatry and Related Sciences, 38(1), 58-68.

Khaleque, A., & Rohner, R. P. (2002). Perceived parental acceptance-rejection and psychological adjustment: A meta-analysis of cross-cultural and intracultural studies. Journal of Marriage and Family, 64(1), 54-64.

Kim, O. M., Reichwald, R., & Lee, R. (2013). Cultural socialization in families with adopted Korean adolescents: A mixed-method, multi-informant study. Journal of Adolescent Research, 28(1), 69-95.

Leary, J. D. (2001). A dissertation on African American male youth violence: "Trying to kill the part of you that isn't loved." Unpublished doctoral dissertation, Portland State University.

Li, Y., Costanzo, P. R., & Putalllaz, M. (2010). Maternal socialization goals, parenting styles, and social-emotional adjustment among Chinese and European American young adults: Testing a mediation model. The Journal of Genetic Psychology, 171(4), 330-362.

Littlejohn-Blake, S. M., & Carol, A. (1993). Understanding the strengths of African American families. Journal of Black Studies, 23(4), 460-471.

Loury, G. C. (1998). An American tragedy: The legacy of slavery lingers in our cities' ghettos. The Brookings Review, 16(2), 38-42. doi:10.2307/20080781

Mckee, A. (2003). *Textual analysis: A beginner's guide.* Thousand Oaks, CA: SAGE Publications.

Meltzoff, A. N. (1999). Born to learn: What infants learn from watching us. Fox, L. A. Leavitt, & J. G. Warhol (Eds.), Pediatric Round Table Series (pp. 145-164). Skillman, NJ: Pediatric Institute Publications.

Nagata, D. K. (Spring 1991). Transgenerational impact of the Japanese

American Internment: Clinical issues in working with children of former internees. Psychotherapy, 28(1), pp. 121-128.

Nichols, E. J. (1976). Introduction to the axiological model. World Psychiatric Association and the Nigerian Association of Psychiatrists. University of Ibadan, Nigeria.

Orellana , M. F., & Bowman, P. (2003). Cultural diversity research on learning and development: Conceptual, methodological, and strategic considerations. Educational Researcher, 32(5), 26-32.

Nyame, K. (2016). The relationship between discipline practices and cultural socialization among African Americans. Thesis (Ed. D.) --University of Rochester. Margaret Warner Graduate School of Education and Human Development, 2016. http://hdl.handle.net/1802/31126

Patton, S. (2007). *That mean old yesterday.* (Vol. 200). Simon and Schuster.

Porter, M. E., & Kramer, M. R. (2002). The competitive advantage of corporate philanthropy. Harvard Business Review, 80(12), 56-68.

Poussaint, A. F., & Alexander, A. (2000). *Lay my burden down.* Boston: Beacon Press.

Powell, J. A., & Spencer, M. L. (2003). Giving them the old "one-two": gentrification and the K.O. of improvised urban dwellers of color. Howard Law Review, 46, 433-490.

Rabaka, R. (2007). The souls of white folk: WEB Du Bois's critique of white supremacy and contributions to critical white studies. The Journal of African American Studies, 11(1), 1-15.

Rogers, D. (2003). Diversity training: good for business but insufficient for social change. In W. S. Center, Dismantling Racism: A Resource Book (pp. 6-8). Portland, OR.

Rogoff, B., & Morelli, G. (1989). Perspectives on children's development from cultural psychology. American Psychologist, 44, 343-348.

Stangor, C. (2004). *Research methods for the behavioral* sciences (2nd Ed.). Boston, MA: Houghton Mifflin.

Stamm, B. H., Stamm IV, H. E., Hudnall, A. C., & Higson-Smith, C. (2004). Considering a theory of cultural trauma and loss. Journal of Loss and Trauma: International Perspectives on Stress & Coping, 9(1), 89-111.

Sztompka, P. (2000). Cultural trauma the other face of social change. European Journal of Social Theory, 3(4), 449-466.

Tatum, B. D. (1997). *"Why are all the black kids sitting together in the cafeteria?" and other conversations about race.* New York: Basic Books.

Taylor, J., & Grundy, C. (1996). *Measuring Black internalization of white stereotypes about African Americans: The Nadanolitization Scale.* In R. L. Jones (Ed.), Handbook of tests and measurements for Black Populations. (Vol. 2, pp. 217-226). Hampton, VA: Cobb & Henry.

Thomas, A. J., & Speight, S. L. (1999). Racial identity and racial socialization attitudes of African American parents. Journal of Black Psychology, 25, 152-170.

Thomas, A. J., Speight, S. L., & Witherspoon, K. M. (2010). Racial socialization, racial identity, and race-related stress of African American parents. The Family Journal: Counseling and Therapy for Couples and Families, 18(4), 407-412a.

Thomas, E. M. (2000). Parental perceptions of the effective Black parenting program. Walden University. ProQuest Dissertations and Theses.

U.S. Census Bureau (2012). New York State area demographics. Retrieved from http://quickfacts.census.gov/qfd/states/36/3663000.html/

Van der Kolk, B. A. (1989). The compulsion to repeat the trauma. Re-enactment, revictimization, and masochism. Psychiatric Clinics of North America, 12(2), 389-411.

Vygotsky, L. S. (1978). *Mind and Society: The development of higher mental processes*. Cambridge, MA: Harvard University Press.

Wesley-Esquimaux, C. C., & Smolewski, M. (2004). *Historic trauma and aboriginal healing.* Ottawa, Ontario: The Aboriginal Healing Foundation.

White-Johnson, R. L., Ford, K. R., & Sellers, R. M. (2010). Parental racial socialization profiles: Association with demographic factors, racial discrimination, childhood socialization, and racial identity. Cultural Diversity and Ethnic Minority Psychology, 16(2), 237-247.

Woodson, C. G. (1990). *The mis-education of the Negro*. 1933. Trenton, NJ: Africa. World Press.

ABOUT THE AUTHOR

KIAH E. NYAME, Ed.D, CPE, LPC.

Dr. Nyame is a national and international speaker and trainer. He provides for profit and non profit organizations with trainings, organizational change, relationship models, and equity & justice management.

He specializes in coaching executive leaders and individuals impacted by post and contemporary traumas. Providing individuals and families with counseling education and healing processes, focused on personal development, socio-cultural and generational traumas.

Dr. Nyame states that his greatest passion is to bring children and families that have experienced traumatic and/or stressful social and cultural events, to a place of finding wellness. Helping individuals, families, and diverse groups develop healthy relationships and find common human connections that strengthen harmonious racial and cultural differences. Dr. Nyame's focus is the betterment and well-being and healing of the human existence.

He serves as Founding Executive Director of Ujima Rochester/Ujima Atlanta, Inc. from January 2002- present. Ujima is a pro-social development agency serving severely-at-risk youth and their families. In 2011 Dr. Nyame created the African World History Classes in Rochester and Atlanta to support lay-persons, youth, human service, and education professionals increase knowledge of the historical contributions of the African Diaspora. Dr. Nyame serves as a Social-Justice and Program Evaluation Consultant, as well as a Cultural & Social Trauma Educator. In 1997 he co-founded, Umoja n Recovery a chemical dependency recovery group dealing with issues specific to African Americans. He has served as a founding member of the Rochester Fatherhood Resource Initiative Inc. and has served as an Effective Black Parenting and Family Consultant and Young Men's and Young Women's Rites of Passage curriculum developer and trainer. Dr. Kiah E. Nyame has more than twenty years of experience in the education, juvenile justice, and youth behavioral fields. His expertise is in family, youth, and generational cultural trauma and youth intervention and prevention. Dr. Nyame is a Licensed Professional Counselor, Certified Executive Leadership Coach, Certified Program Evaluator, and an Organizational Equity Transformation Consultant.

Dr. Nyame has researched and presented workshops and trainings on cultural trauma, youth social development, family, community, and school collaborations, social justice & equity, and gangs and violence as a result of social-trauma. Some of his work includes;

Presenter/Trainer focused on Understanding Trauma & Stress on Parenting and avoiding re-injury at North America Family Institute's Therapeutic Foster Care Training on August 14, 2017 & August 26, 2017.

Invited Presenter/Trainer focused on

Impact of Trauma and Stress on Parenting at Rochester City School District's MBK Summer Parent Workshop Series on July 25 & 27, 2017.

Invited Presenter on topic of *I Don't Even See Race* at the University of Rochester Medical Center's Psychiatric Department 5th Annual Summer Brown Bag Series on July 20th, 2017.

Invited Presenter focused on Healing the Social-Cultural Trauma within Human Service and Educational Systems at the University of Rochester Annual Diversity Conference on March 31, 2017. Medaille College-Rochester lecture on Characteristics of Multi-cultural Counseling on January 22, 2017 and May 21, 2017.

Invited Presenter: Healing the Trauma; Empowering Our Youth. Invited to give a guest lecture at Nazareth College, Institute for Pluralism Rochester, N. Y. Lecture: *Are we post-racial America? Cultural Specific Models of Service and Delivery* at the City of Rochester Training Conference, Rochester, NY. Dr. Nyame considers his invitation as International Guest Panelist: Université Cheikh Anta Diop (FASTEF) Dakar, Senegal, West Africa, his flagship presentation to date.

Along with serving as the Graduate Student Commencement Speaker for St. John Fisher College. Dr. Kiah Nyame is the creator of "A Time for Healing, Educating & Rebuilding; Exploring the socio-cultural trauma and stigma of the urban community", training conferences since 2009.

His current Research focus is on *How Parents Impacted by Socio-Cultural Trauma, Socialize Their Children and the Generational Influence.*

Dr. Nyame completed his Doctoral Degree in Counseling & Human Development at the University of Rochester's Warner School of Education. He completed his Master's Degree in Human Service Administration at St. John Fisher College.

MORE ABOUT THE AUTHOR...

"Dr. Kiah Nyame, affectionately known as Dr. K, shares details of his private life whereas most would internalize such details to the point of devastation. His search for truth and desire to heal have helped him surpass unbelievable odds. These experiences, along with his academic achievements, make him an authentic advocate for those effected by traumatic life experiences."

-Terry Chaka, Artist,
Executive Director
The Baobab Cultural Center.

"Coming to know Dr. Nyame has been a blessing in The Afrikan Village & Cultural Center. We always knew he was a valuable asset to the collective of our people, but we were not fully aware of the traumatic experiences he navigated through. After reading his book, I gained a deeper level of respect and honor for who and what he is. As you read this book, I am sure that the impact on your life will become a platform for encouragement, inspiration, and strengthening. I am so thankful for the divine efficacy that allowed our paths to cross."

- Dr. Ray Hagins,
Chief Elder
The Afrikan Village
& Cultural Center

"Dr. Kiah Nyame is a healer... one that embodies the spirit, techniques, and character of our ancient ancestors. This book and its contents bring forth his testimony and a healing offering to the growing need for mental and spiritual wellbeing. I have had a front row seat to the last 10 years of Dr. K's journey to the ranks of healers; a journey that has continuously evolved. The imagery and truth presented here is an invitation to visit your own journey in the hopes that you too can heal and or continue the evolution of healing. Ma'at Hotep."

-Jerome Underwood
CEO, Action for a Better Community, Inc.

ACKNOWLEDGMENTS

First, I'd like to thank the Creator. Reaching this point would not have been possible without the help and support of many people along the way. I would like to thank some by name. Thank you to my dissertation committee: To Dr. Dena Phillips Swanson, for advising me and challenging me to grow as a researcher, personally, and professionally.

I would also like to acknowledge a list of extended family members, friends, colleagues, and mentors, who have contributed to my personal success directly or indirectly: Bro. Avery T. Blackman, Queen Mother Iris Banister, My Sister Carol "Coco" Simpson, Sis Nzinga, Dr. Hussain & Hannah Ahmed, Sundiata & Nzingha Sheppard, and the entire AFFANTE for guiding me towards the greatness of my heritage, the importance of honoring my elders and ancestors, and learning to see greatness in myself.

To Dr. Joy Angela DeGruy, Dr. Ray Hagins, Dr. Molefi Kete Asante, and Dr. Babacar Falls for friendship, challenging me, and most of all for being teachers of truth. Maat Hetep.

To Dr. Frederick Jefferson and the Cohort XIII members of the Leadership Coaching Certificate Program for their belief and support of this work.

Finally, I must acknowledge my Rochester and world-wide 12-Step family for helping to order my Steps, my many friends and acquaintances, and all those whose paths I've crossed along life's journey.

Made in the USA
Middletown, DE
05 July 2020